Copyright © 2020 by Heather Chancellor. All rights reserved.

The A-Z of Christian Living. First Edition. Cover Photo & Design Copyright © Mimika Cooney

Ebook ISBN 978-1-7343520-6-1. Print ISBN 979-8-9873949-7-7.

No part of this publication may be reproduced, stored or transmitted in any form or by any means, electronic, mechanical, photocopying, recording, scanning, or otherwise without written permission from the publisher. It is illegal to copy this book, post it to a website, or distribute it by any other means without permission.

The author has no responsibility for the persistence or accuracy of URLs for external or third-party Internet Websites referred to in this publication and does not guarantee that any content on such Websites is, or will remain, accurate or appropriate.

Unless otherwise indicated, all Scripture quotations are taken from the Holy Bible, New International Version®, NIV®. Copyright ©1973, 1978, 1984, 2011 by Biblica, Inc.™. The "NIV" and "New International Version" are trademarks registered in the United States Patent and Trademark Office by Biblica, Inc.™

While every attempt has been made to verify information provided in this book, the author assumes no responsibility for any errors, inaccuracies or omissions. If advice concerning medical matters is needed, the services of a qualified professional should be sought. This book is not intended for use as a source of medical advice. The examples within the book are not intended to represent or guarantee that anyone will achieve their desired results. Each individuals success will be determined by his or her desire, dedication, effort and motivation.

The author has made the stylistic choice to capitalize certain words and pronouns that refer to the Father, Son, Holy Spirit, Christ, although it may differ from the stylistic choices of other publishers. For spelling purposes the use of British English is used throughout.

This book and all other materials is published by Mimika Media LLC.

Contents

Invitation	V
1. A Thought	1
2. A Message	2
3. Blessings	3
4. Boldness	4
5. Christian Life	5
6. Conflicts	6
7. Discernment	7
8. Every Way of The Test	8
9. Faith	9
10. Fruit of The Spirit	10
11. Glorify God	11
12. God Allows What We Allow	12
13. God's Rest	13
14. Grace	14
15. Harmony	15
16. In God's Will	16

17.	Jesus Helps Us Overcome	17
18.	Joy	18
19.	Keys of Five	19
20.	Let Our Light Shine	20
21.	Living Sacrifice	21
22.	Love	22
23.	Love and Kindness	23
24.	My King	24
25.	My Way	25
26.	Need of The Spirit	26
27.	Our Covenant	27
28.	Prayers	28
29.	Question Your Obedience	29
30.	Rungs on The Ladder	30
31.	Special Love	31
32.	The Holy Trinity	32
33.	Time	33
34.	Understanding The Lord's Prayer	34
35.	Value Holiness	35
36.	Way of The Christian	36
37.	X - It Of The Elect	37
38.	Yearn For Glory	38
39.	Zero In	39
	About the Author	40

Invitation

Get free book bonuses by visiting www.heatherchancellor.com

Chapter 1

A Thought

Different paths must cross to keep the circle rotating
Moods and tensions providing the cogs in the wheel
Which progresses on the uneven ground
The basic of the movement of situations
Crossing the roads, which traverse
This difficult and meaningful journey
Which must be accomplished to complete
The moving cycle of events protruding
Like harmful rocks along the wayside
Not to be ignored or discarded as
Every imprint is left to remain forever
Whether the traveller has chosen or not
To find assistance in their interruptions
The glass walls are not unpenetrable
When a strong will can force the flow
Of the stream of events in the path
Which must be pursued to the end
As the wall of reality must be faced
Seek and ye shall find the happiness
Which can be enjoyed or destroyed
By the participants unanimous choice
So it should be endeavored to let it be.

Chapter 2

A Message

1 Corinthians 14:2
For anyone who speaks in a tongue does not speak to people but to God. Indeed, no one understands them; they utter mysteries by the Spirit.

When in reverence to God you stand
On you He will rest His hand
And in many tongues and sighs
He will gently lift you on high
And to overflowing His power
On and in you He shall shower
And with His light and breath
You can send away a death
Life here on earth you choose
And many will be lift behind
Because of no control of mind
the time has come for all to see
The wonder of our Holy Majesty

Chapter 3

Blessings

Ephesians 1: 3 -4
3 Blessed *be* the God and Father of our Lord Jesus Christ, who has blessed us with every spiritual blessing in the heavenly *places* in Christ, **4** just as He chose us in Him before the foundation of the world, that we should be holy and without blame before Him in love.

Strive in all to be perfect
The blessings will be worth it
God's love passes all understanding
As His blessings you are handling
Which pour out from above
From His Holy Spiritual love.

Chapter 4
Boldness

Ephesians 3: 11-12
11 according to the eternal purpose which He accomplished in Christ Jesus our Lord, **12** in whom we have boldness and access with confidence through faith in Him.

Nothing will remain the same
As you grow in Jesus's name
And your spirit becomes bold
As you onto the Holy Spirit hold
Climbing rocks and mountains high
Then you reach to the sky.

Chapter 5

Christian Life

Romans 8: 38
[38] For I am persuaded that neither death nor life, nor angels nor principalities nor powers, nor things present nor things to come.

Being a Christian is not easy
Sometimes you can feel queasy
Because the world system is unfair It tries to trap like a lion's liar.
But in the midst of all is a table
Prepared by God for us to label
All those around us who try
To confuse and mislead us by lies.
But we learn to walk in God's strength
As he takes us from length to length
To obtain the ultimate balance
Which is the Christian's challenge.

Chapter 6

Conflicts

James 1: 2-4

2 My brethren, count it all joy when you fall into various trials, **3** knowing that the testing of your faith produces patience. **4** But let patience have *its* perfect work, that you may be perfect and complete, lacking nothing.

As we meet our conflicts
Our reactions make us sick
And we assess in the battle
Importance of what we prattle.
We will begin to realise
That there is no compromise
In Jesus's way of responding
To situations we are bonding.

Chapter 7

Discernment

Ephesians 6: 12-17

12 For we do not wrestle against flesh and blood, but against principalities, against powers, against the rulers of the darkness of this age, against spiritual *hosts* of wickedness in the heavenly *places.* **13** Therefore take up the whole armor of God, that you may be able to withstand in the evil day, and having done all, to stand. **14** Stand therefore, having girded your waist with truth, having put on the breastplate of righteousness, **15** and having shod your feet with the preparation of the gospel of peace; **16** above all, taking the shield of faith with which you will be able to quench all the fiery darts of the wicked one. **17** And take the helmet of salvation, and the sword of the Spirit, which is the word of God.

You can in peace live
And to others always give
Nothing will put you down
As on Satan you frown.
Cut Satan from your life
With God's Spiritual knife
And from you he will flee
As you with new eyes see.

Chapter 8

Every Way of The Test

James 1: 8
8 *he is* a double-minded man, unstable in all his ways.

While angels look after you daily
As you with your life go on gaily
And your stomach to the top fill
God does not go against your will
As you all pleasures seek and find
And do not discipline your mind
But enjoy drink, food and song
All the days and nights long
Then God will put you to the test
And you will not have done your best.

Chapter 9

Faith

Hebrews 11:6
6 But without faith *it is* impossible to please *Him,* for he who comes to God must believe that He is, and *that* He is a rewarder of those who diligently seek Him.

We are in the way, not on the way
To pleasing God in all every day
Persecution and trials will you refine
So you become pure as gold in mind.
Our inheritance from above is imperishable
As suffering here is only temporal
From faith is salvation of our soul
As we as Christians fulfill our role.

Chapter 10

Fruit of The Spirit

Galatians 5: 22-23
[22] But the fruit of the Spirit is love, joy, peace, long suffering, kindness, goodness, faithfulness, [23] gentleness, self-control. Against such there is no law.

My spirit to you I hand over
White like the Cliffs of Dover
Feeling your strength at night
I stand in your brilliant light.
My spirit begins to soar
As you open all the doors
To Love, Joy, Meekness and Kindness
Faith, Hope, Peace and Goodness.

Chapter 11

Glorify God

Psalms 144: 1-2

[1] Blessed *be* the Lord my Rock, Who trains my hands for war, *And* my fingers for battle [2] My lovingkindness and my fortress, My high tower and my deliverer, My shield and *the One* in whom I take refuge, Who subdues my people under me.

My children, says the Lord, I will protect
If the world's ways you do reject
I will surround you with a wall
Against which Satan's wiles will fall.
Forgiveness must be in your heart
So in my Kingdom you do your part
Then my works will be known
And my gifts to all shown.
So my name will be glorified
And through this, wrongs rectified.

Chapter 12

God Allows What We Allow

Matthew 16: 19
¹⁹ And I will give you the keys of the kingdom of heaven, and whatever you bind on earth will be bound in heaven, and whatever you loose on earth will be loosed in heaven."

God is our Heavenly source
Of our energetic inner force
And it is for us to allow
What we will in our life plough
And God gives us free will
As to what our spirit we fill.
So we are made in His likeness
So we can walk in His kindness
And Satan's power is but a whisper
As to God's powerful thunder
Good or bad is said with our tongue
As are God's praises easily sung.
So Jesus's way we can accept
Or all his examples reject
We can make the right decision
To live our life to the precision
Of walking in God's given power
Which over Satan will tower.

Chapter 13

God's Rest

Hebrews 4: 1
Therefore, since a promise remains of entering His rest, let us fear lest any of you seem to have come short of it.

Lord I rest in your caring
My life with you I am sharing
My spirit to you I am baring
As I become bold and daring.
You add to my life the best
As I try to pass the test
Satan's tempting me in jest
But in your arms I rest.

Chapter 14

Grace

2 Corinthians 3: 17-18
17 Now the Lord is the Spirit; and where the Spirit of the Lord *is*, there *is* liberty. **18** But we all, with unveiled face, beholding as in a mirror the glory of the Lord, are being transformed into the same image from glory to glory, just as by the Spirit of the Lord.

God pours down His special love
From His high heavenly home above
In God's grace we do walk
As we daily with Him talk
If we do not the spirit grieve
We spiritually will be free.

Chapter 15

Harmony

Ephesians 3: 20
[20] Now to Him who is able to do exceedingly abundantly above all that we ask or think, according to the power that works in us.

I am surrounded by a bubble
Which increases my blessings double
Of Joy, Peace, Love and Harmony
And I give thanks to God in psalmody.
The bubble surrounds me each day
As in reverence I stand and pray
And His energy on me He pours
As I walk according to his laws.

Chapter 16

In God's Will

1 Peter 5: 6
6 Therefore humble yourselves under the mighty hand of God, that He may exalt you in due time.

A tender heart and a humble mind
Courtesy, and to all to be kind
Is in the ability of always giving
To all as of God you are receiving
When you feel down with rejection
You assume you have no protection.
But for God you to use
Mercy and Love you must choose
And to all prove the Gospel
As fears and doubts you distill
And in your faith walk you prevail
In God's Will you will not fail.

Chapter 17

Jesus Helps Us Overcome

1 Peter 5: 7-10

[7] casting all your care upon Him, for He cares for you. [8] Be sober, be vigilant; because your adversary the devil walks about like a roaring lion, seeking whom he may devour. [9] Resist him, steadfast in the faith, knowing that the same sufferings are experienced by your brotherhood in the world. [10] But may the God of all grace, who called us to His eternal glory by Christ Jesus, after you have suffered a while, perfect, establish, strengthen, and settle *you*.

Joyfully we sing out aloud
That of Jesus we are proud
Gratefully we receive His Grace
In this difficult earthy race.
In Jesus our sorrows we hide
Walking with Him at our side
Satan around us tries to roar
But we firmly close the door.
We push Satan right down
So Jesus's blessings will us crown
As we receive His special love
From the Holy fountains above.

Chapter 18

Joy

Nehemiah 8: 10
10 Then he said to them, "Go your way, eat the fat, drink the sweet, and send portions to those for whom nothing is prepared; for *this* day *is* holy to our Lord. Do not sorrow, for the joy of the Lord is your strength."

When my Holy Lord I have sought
My joy is a bubble bursting forth
Up and out of all of me
For all people to feel and see
You must do things on your own
So good works will be sown
The result will be the best
For those who pass the test
Times are short for Christ to come
And all your works to have done.

Chapter 19

Keys of Five

Romans 8: 26-27

26 Likewise the Spirit also helps in our weaknesses. For we do not know what we should pray for as we ought, but the Spirit Himself makes intercession for us with groanings which cannot be uttered. **27** Now He who searches the hearts knows what the mind of the Spirit *is*, because He makes intercession for the saints according to *the will of God.*

As we pray to our Father on High
Our spirits fill and we begin to sigh
The Holy Spirit for our needs intercedes
For everyone and you and me.
Our spirit man we build up and edify
As we our Father humbly glorify
We offer up our thanks with praise
As our spirits to Heaven raise.
With prayers we our faith increase
And our spirits fill with inner peace
Then we understand mysteries on high
As we to our Father draw nigh.

Chapter 20

Let Our Light Shine

Matthew 5: 16
16 Let your light so shine before men, that they may see your good works and glorify your Father in heaven.

May your spiritual light
Shine through with might
People to us God will send
And their hearts can mend
As they Jesus in us see
And to him bend their knee
Light will shine through darkness
As people see our kindness.

Chapter 21

Living Sacrifice

Romans 12: 1
I beseech you therefore, brethren, by the mercies of God, that you present your bodies a living sacrifice, holy, acceptable to God, *which is* your reasonable service.

Give your body as a living sacrifice
And forget about all things nice
As you daily in God's Will stand
He will lead you by your hand.
Giving thanks in all is the key
To communication with our Majesty
He will open or close many doors
As you go about your daily chores.

Chapter 22

Love

John 3: 16
16 For God so loved the world that He gave His only begotten Son, that whoever believes in Him should not perish but have everlasting life.

We always think about Love
Which comes from God above
Continuously we talk about Love
Which from us flies like a dove
Always we try to understand Love
Which covers us like a glove.
God showed us Love is a sacrifice
Of something very special and nice
Love is unconditional to any
Asking nothing in return for many
Love rises up from deep inside
And cannot our feelings hide.
Love is the most beautiful thing
That makes us want to sing
And give it to one another
Like a child and a mother
Without Love you are nothing
For your spirit needs it to ring.

Chapter 23

Love and Kindness

1 Corinthians 13: 8
8 Love never fails. But whether *there are* prophecies, they will fail; whether *there are* tongues, they will cease; whether *there is* knowledge, it will vanish away.

Love and Kindness go together
With which you can measure
The Holy Spirit within you
Who daily keeps you new.
He comforts and guides your life
And cuts Satan like a knife
And his power pours out
And eradicates all doubt.

Chapter 24

My King

John 14: 13-14

[13] And whatever you ask in My name, that I will do, that the Father may be glorified in the Son. [14] If you ask anything in My name, I will do *it*.

I am very proud
To say out aloud
That Jesus is my King
And with joy I sing
That I have no fear
For all bondages disappear
When the name above all
On Satan's ears fall.

Chapter 25

My Way

Deuteronomy 28:47
47 "Because you did not serve the Lord your God with joy and gladness of heart, for the abundance of everything.

In my temple there is sin
So many souls I cannot win
I will add that I will add
So that My Will will be had.
I will remove what I will remove
When and whom I will choose
So to the side I will lay
And put to rest all the day.
For my powers must now be shown
For all spiritually to have grown
In my ways for all to see
Love and healing received from me.

Chapter 26

Need of The Spirit

Psalms 144: 1-2

[1] Blessed *be* the Lord my Rock, Who trains my hands for war, *And* my fingers for battle— [2] My lovingkindness and my fortress, My high tower and my deliverer, My shield and *the One* in whom I take refuge, Who subdues my people under me.

We thank you for your power
Which all can use like a tower
Of strength to fill our spirit
Aiding us to pass tests with merit
Thank you for this special gift
Which us to the Heaven's lift.

Chapter 27

Our Covenant

James 1: 2-3
2 My brethren, count it all joy when you fall into various trials, **3** knowing that the testing of your faith produces patience.

Jesus was sent for us to see
How we should act and be
A Covenant with God was made
With conditions as how to behave
Which were based on true love
Sent down from God above
Jesus showed us how to overcome
All trials and test to have won.

Chapter 28

Prayers

Matthew 21:22
22 And whatever things you ask in prayer, believing, you will receive.

Your prayers are you life line
For God to see in your mind
Requesting what you want to do
He sends his Angels around you to
Arrange and show you a sign
That all things will turn out fine
As you in reverence to him pray
He will add all things to your day.

Chapter 29

Question Your Obedience

Colossians 3: 1-3
[1] If then you were raised with Christ, seek those things which are above, where Christ is, sitting at the right hand of God.
[2] Set your mind on things above, not on things on the earth.
[3] For you died, and your life is hidden with Christ in God.

Come to Jesus, before Him kneel
And your Covenant with Him seal
Live in all in total obedience
And on you He will bestow lenience
Then in all things of the earth
You will look at with mirth
Understanding confines of the rules
Rewards will be added like jewels.

Chapter 30

Rungs on The Ladder

Luke 6: 37-38

[37] "Judge not, and you shall not be judged. Condemn not, and you shall not be condemned. Forgive, and you will be forgiven. [38] Give, and it will be given to you: good measure, pressed down, shaken together, and running over will be put into your bosom. For with the same measure that you use, it will be measured back to you."

We look about to seek and find
Things which stick like glue to bind
Forgetting the essence of life is giving
And to all total and absolute forgiving
Then in God's arms you will rest
And He will add all things best.

Chapter 31

Special Love

Ephesians 2: 6-7

6 and raised *us* up together, and made *us* sit together in the heavenly *places* in Christ Jesus, **7** that in the ages to come He might show the exceeding riches of His grace in *His* kindness toward us in Christ Jesus.

Our Lord God sits in Heaven
His special number is seven
He looks down on us below
As we about our chores do go
He hopes good works we will sow
And others Jesus in us will know.

Chapter 32

The Holy Trinity

John 14: 25-26

²⁵ "These things I have spoken to you while being present with you. ²⁶ But the Helper, the Holy Spirit, whom the Father will send in My name, He will teach you all things, and bring to your remembrance all things that I said to you.

Father, Son and Spirit are the Trinity,
They reign now and for Eternity
God is our wonderful Heavenly Father
Whose Love surrounds us like a lather.
Jesus is our example, guide and friend
And He from above Angels to us send
The Holy Spirit comforts us from within
And with Wisdom helps us to fight Sin.

Chapter 33

Time

James 4: 14
14 whereas you do not know what *will happen* tomorrow. For what *is* your life? It is even a vapor that appears for a little time and then vanishes away.

There was no such thing as time
For us to understand the shine
Of things to be that He makes
So God allowed it for our sakes.
We have been given our life time
Which is as quick as a chime
God's time always stands still
We use it according to our will.

Chapter 34

Understanding The Lord's Prayer

Matthew 6: 9-14

⁹ In this manner, therefore, pray: Our Father in heaven, Hallowed be Your name. ¹⁰ Your kingdom come. Your will be done On earth as *it is* in heaven. ¹¹ Give us this day our daily bread. ¹² And forgive us our debts, As we forgive our debtors. ¹³ And do not lead us into temptation, But deliver us from the evil one. For Yours is the kingdom and the power and the glory forever. Amen. ¹⁴ For if you forgive men their trespasses, your heavenly Father will also forgive you.

The Lord's Prayer is the key
As you reverence His Majesty
Then your inner spirit will soar
As He opens up the door
To love, Joy, Peace and Kindness
As you pray to Him in likeness.

Chapter 35

Value Holiness

1 Peter 1: 14-16

14 as obedient children, not conforming yourselves to the former lusts, *as* in your ignorance; **15** but as He who called you *is* holy, you also be holy in all *your* conduct, **16** because it is written, "Be holy, for I am holy."

Satan attacks you in your mind
And if you hide things he will bind
So sober and vigilant you must stay
As you fight for right in this fray.
And base your hope on God's grace
And peace will shine from your face
Stay Holy in all your conduct
And Faith will be the product.
Conduct yourself in God's way
And to Him draw near without delay
God says "You shall be Holy"
As He says "For I am Holy".

Chapter 36

Way of The Christian

1 Corinthians 9: 26-27

26 Therefore I run thus: not with uncertainty. Thus I fight: not as *one who* beats the air. **27** But I discipline my body and bring *it* into subjection, lest, when I have preached to others, I myself should become disqualified.

You can be meek and bold
As chapters in your life unfold.
You can be humble and strong
And that is right not wrong.
You can be kind and assertive
Not bossy and always negative.
Physical works must be done
For spirits have to be won.
The Angels will be there to lead
As earthy beings have their need.

Chapter 37

X – It Of The Elect

Matthew 24: 30-31
30 Then the sign of the Son of Man will appear in heaven, and then all the tribes of the earth will mourn, and they will see the Son of Man coming on the clouds of heaven with power and great glory. **31** And He will send His angels with a great sound of a trumpet, and they will gather together His elect from the four winds, from one end of heaven to the other.

You are the Christ and Lord
Who all blessings give and hoard
For the time when we do come
And good works for you have done.
You fill up my very being
And with your eyes I am seeing
The glory that awaits us soon
When you triumphantly arrive at noon.
We praise your very special name
As we learn our tongues to tame
You are the Rose of Sharon
Without whom my life is barren.

Chapter 38

Yearn For Glory

1 Corinthians 15: 40
40 *There are* also celestial bodies and terrestrial bodies; but the glory of the celestial *is* one, and the *glory* of the terrestrial *is* another.

Our body is a blessing from above
And we must treat it with love
As the Holy Spirit in us resides
But also lusts of the flesh hides.
Satan will deceive you with lies
And try to make you compromise
But there is only one way
And that is to walk with Jesus all day.

Chapter 39

Zero In

Matthew 6: 33
33 But seek first the kingdom of God and His righteousness, and all these things shall be added to you.

Patch all the holes
That tunnel us like moles
Trying to find the way
To see the light of day.
Those living under the law
Will see much more
Of God's way every day
As you to him pray.

About the Author

Heather Chancellor is a South African born British writer. Having lived in three countries, she has seen the hand of God throughout her life in many experiences. She loves to share her heart for God's love. Heather has two adult daughters and four grandchildren. She lives in York, England.
https://www.heatherchancellor.com

www.ingramcontent.com/pod-product-compliance
Lightning Source LLC
LaVergne TN
LVHW051205080426
835508LV00021B/2824

LIFTING THE VEIL:

TRANSITIONING FROM A MINISTRY TO BUSINESS MINDSET

PRESENTED BY

LINDA D. LEE, PCLC, CCM

Award-winning author of *In Bed with a Snake*

LIFTING THE VEIL: TRANSITIONING FROM A MINISTRY TO BUSINESS MINDSET

Copyright © 2018 Linda D. Lee

All Rights Reserved.

No part of this book may be reproduced, distributed or transmitted in any form by any means, graphics, electronics, or mechanical, including photocopy, recording, taping, or by any information storage or retrieval system, without permission in writing from the publisher, except in the case of reprints in the context of reviews, quotes, or references. Request for permission should be addressed in writing to LL Media Group, LLC; Attn: Linda D. Lee, CEO; P.O. Box 6305, Fort Worth, TX 76115.

Scripture quotations marked (NKJV) are taken from the Holman Study Bible NKJV Edition, Copyright © 2013. Used by the permission of Holman Bible Publishers, Inc., Nashville, Tennessee. All rights reserved.

Printed in the United States of America

ISBN 13: 978-0-9979068-3-7

A good leader must be:

Strong – Enduring

Mature – Teachable

Obedient – Humble and submissive

Table of Content

	Acknowledgments	i
1	Introduction	Pg 01
2	Was Blind But Now I See	Pg 05
	Exercise	Pg 07
3	Restored to Sanity	Pg 09
	Exercise	Pg 11
4	Never Give Up	Pg 13
	Exercise	Pg 15
5	Accepting the Call	Pg 17
	Exercise	Pg 19
	Meet the Authors	Pg 28